Reading: Informational Text Learning Stations Grades 6–8

English Language Arts series

Authors:	Schyrlet Cameron and Suzanne Myers
Editors:	Mary Dieterich and Sarah M. Anderson
Proofreader:	Margaret Brown

COPYRIGHT © 2013 Mark Twain Media, Inc.

ISBN 978-1-62223-003-7

Printing No. CD-404178

Mark Twain Media, Inc., Publishers
Distributed by Carson-Dellosa Publishing LLC

The purchase of this book entitles the buyer to reproduce the student pages for classroom use only. Other permissions may be obtained by writing Mark Twain Media, Inc., Publishers.

All rights reserved. Printed in the United States of America.

Visit us at www.carsondellosa.com

Table of Contents

To the Teacher 1
Common Core State Standards Matrix 2

Unit: Inferences and Evidence
Teacher Page 3
Activities
Station One: *Citing Textual Evidence* 4
Station Two: *Evaluating Textual Evidence* ... 5
Station Three: *Making Inferences: Poster* ... 6
Station Four: *Making Inferences and
   Citing Evidence* 7
Handouts
The Nation Mobilizes for War 8
We Can Do It! Poster 9
To the Women of Mobile 10

Unit: Propaganda Techniques
Teacher Page 11
Activities
Station One: *Presidential Campaign
   Commercial, 1952* 12
Station Two: *Presidential Campaign
   Commercial, 1960* 13
Station Three: *Presidential Campaign
   Commercial, 1968* 14
Station Four: *Presidential Campaign
   Commercial, 1984* 15
Station Five: *Presidential Campaign
   Commercial, 2004* 16
Handouts
Propaganda Techniques 17

Unit: Organizational Text Structures
Teacher Page 18
Activities
Station One: *Cause and Effect* 19
Station Two: *Sequential Order* 20
Station Three: *Compare and Contrast* 21
Station Four: *Problem and Solution* 22
Station Five: *Chronological Order* 23
Station Six: *Description* 24
Handouts
*Common Organizational Text
   Structures* 25

Unit: Text Features
Teacher Page 26
Activities
Station One: *Organizational Text
   Features* 27
Station Two: *Print Features* 28
Station Three: *Text Mapping* 29
Station Four: *Graphic Text Features* 30

Unit: Bias and Point of View
Teacher Page 31
Activities
Station One: *Bias* 32
Station Two: *Loaded Words* 33
Station Three: *Point of View* 34
Station Four: *Bias and Point of View* 35
Handout
*Letter to John D. Johnston. Shelbyville.
   November 4, 1851* 36

Unit: Comparing Text and Media
Teacher Page 37
Activities
Station One: *Public Speaking: Tone* 38
Station Two: *Public Speaking: Mood* 39
Station Three: *Evaluation of
   Media Types* 40
Station Four: *Nonverbal Communication* .. 41
Handout
*John F. Kennedy Inaugural Address,
   January 20, 1961 (Transcript)* 42

Answer Keys 45

To the Teacher

In the *English Language Arts* (ELA) *series*, students in grades six through eight explore reading, writing, and language in a learning station environment. Learning stations engage students in individual or small group activities. Learning stations are an instructional strategy that can be used to target specific skills.

Each book in the ELA series features five or six units of study. Each unit has a teacher page that identifies the goal, states the standards, lists materials and setup for the activities, and provides instructions to be presented to students. Also, there are questions for opening discussion and student reflection. (Note: It is important for the teacher to introduce, model, or review the concepts or skills with the students at the beginning of each unit.)

Books in the ELA Series

- *Reading: Literature Learning Stations, Grades 6–8*
  The units focus on alliteration, rhyme, plot and setting, tone and mood, and poetry.

- *Reading: Informational Text Learning Stations, Grades 6–8*
  The units focus on citing evidence, bias, point of view, propaganda techniques, organizational text structures, and text features.

- *Writing Learning Stations, Grades 6–8*
  The units focus on fact and opinion, characterization, making inferences, proofreading, and dialogue.

- *Language Learning Stations, Grades 6–8*
  The units focus on punctuation, dictionary usage, figurative language, roots and affixes, and word meaning.

Reading: Informational Text Learning Stations, Grades 6–8, contains six units of study. Each unit consists of four to six learning station activities. The activity at each station is designed to create interest, provide practice, and stimulate discussion. These units will help students become better readers of nonfiction informational text as they learn to cite evidence from the text and become aware of the author's bias, point of view, and techniques used to persuade the reader. Students will also learn about different ways text may be organized and the text features that help readers get meaning out of the text they read. Whenever applicable, media/technology and speaking/listening skills are integrated into the activity. Handouts are provided as supplemental resources.

The units of study in the ELA series are meant to supplement or enhance the regular classroom English Language Arts curriculum. The station activities are correlated to the strands of the English Language Arts Common Core State Standards.

Common Core State Standards Matrix

English Language Arts Standards: Reading Informational Text

Units of Study	RI.6.1	RI.6.2	RI.6.3	RI.6.4	RI.6.5	RI.6.6	RI.6.7	RI.6.8	RI.6.9	RI.6.10	RI.7.1	RI.7.2	RI.7.3	RI.7.4	RI.7.5	RI.7.6	RI.7.7	RI.7.8	RI.7.9	RI.7.10	RI.8.1	RI.8.2	RI.8.3	RI.8.4	RI.8.5	RI.8.6	RI.8.7	RI.8.8	RI.8.9	RI.8.10
Inferences and Evidence	X										X										X									
Propaganda Techniques		X										X										X								
Organizational Text Structures					X										X										X					
Text Features					X										X										X					
Bias and Point of View						X										X										X				
Comparing Text and Media							X										X										X			

© Copyright 2010. National Governors Association Center for Best Practices and Council of Chief State School Officers. All right reserved.

Teacher Page

Unit: Inferences and Evidence

Goal: Students will be able to make inferences and cite textual evidence.

Common Core State Standards (CCSS):

6th Grade	7th Grade	8th Grade
RI.6.1. Cite textual evidence to support analysis of what the text says explicitly as well as inferences drawn from the text.	RI.7.1. Cite several pieces of textual evidence to support analysis of what the text says explicitly as well as inferences drawn from the text.	RI.8.1. Cite the textual evidence that most strongly supports an analysis of what the text says explicitly as well as inferences drawn from the text.

© Copyright 2010. National Governors Association Center for Best Practices and Council of Chief State School Officers. All rights reserved.

Materials List/Setup

Station 1: Citing Textual Evidence (Activity); The Nation Mobilizes for War (Handout)
Station 2: Evaluating Textual Evidence (Activity); The Nation Mobilizes for War (Handout)
Station 3*: Making Inferences: Poster (Activity); We Can Do It! Poster (Handout)
Station 4: Making Inferences and Citing Evidence (Activity); To the Women of Mobile (Handout)

Activity: one copy per student
Handout: one copy per each student in a group

*Technology Integration—Station 3: Students can view a color image of the We Can Do It! Poster at <http://media.nara.gov/media/images/20/7/20-0697a.gif>

Opening: Discussion Questions (Teacher-Directed)

1. What do you know about World War II?
2. What do you know about the life on the American home front during World War II? [Possible answers: women joined workforce, rationing, victory gardens]

Student Instructions for Learning Stations

At the learning stations, you will explore the mobilization of the American home front during World War II. Activities will focus on women entering the workforce to support the war effort. You will practice making inferences and citing textual evidence. Discuss your answers with other team members after completing each activity.

Closure: Reflection

The following questions can be used to stimulate discussion or as a journaling activity.
1. Why were women needed to enter the workforce?
2. What jobs were available for women who entered the workforce?
3. How do you think women were affected after the war ended and the men returned home?

Name: _____ Date: _____

Station One: Citing Textual Evidence

Directions: Read the selection "The Nation Mobilizes for War." Cite three pieces of textual evidence that could be used to answer Question A and three pieces of textual evidence that could be used to answer Question B.

> **Question A:** What impact did World War II have on factories and production?

Evidence 1: _____

_____

_____

Evidence 2: _____

_____

_____

Evidence 3: _____

_____

_____

> **Question B:** How did the war change the American labor force?

Evidence 1: _____

_____

_____

Evidence 2: _____

_____

_____

Evidence 3: _____

_____

_____

Name: _____ Date: _____

Station Two: Evaluating Textual Evidence

Directions: Read the selection "The Nation Mobilizes for War." Then read the two questions in the box below. In the graphic organizer, place an X in the first column if the statement could be used as textual evidence for Question 1. Place an X in the second column if the statement could be used as textual evidence for Question 2. Some textual evidence may support both questions. If the statement is not textual evidence for either question, place an X in the NOT column.

Questions

1. Was Japanese Admiral Yamamoto correct when he said, "we have only awakened a sleeping giant, and his reaction will be terrible"?

2. How did President Roosevelt's decisions about military production support his calling the United States, "the arsenal for democracy"?

Question #1	Question #2	Not	Textual Evidence Statement
			A. By a unanimous vote, the Senate voted for war, and only one House member voted against war.
			B. the symbol of the "new woman" was "Rosie the Riveter"
			C. long lines gathered in front of recruiting stations
			D. The president set high, and some said impossible, goals for production, and all of them were exceeded.
			E. and very few Americans did not give it (the war) full support
			F. by 1942, they were turning out products 24 hours a day
			G. Nearly all civilian production stopped so that factories could devote full attention to military needs.
			H. The Office of Price Administration (OPA) was created to keep prices in check.
			I. the 450,000-man military force of 1940 increasing to 9 million in 1943
			J. Factories that had been shut down in 1938 went to eight-hour shifts in 1939

Name: _____ Date: _____

Station Three: Making Inferences: Poster

The "We Can Do It!" poster was used to recruit women into the workforce during World War II. The female character was known as Rosie the Riveter, and she appeared in a variety of recruitment posters.

Directions: An **inference** is your best guess based on evidence and reasoning. Take time to examine the poster. Begin by looking at the poster as a whole. Then focus on the individual details. To answer the questions, make inferences about what you observed.

1. What does the slogan "We Can Do It!" mean?

   _____

   _____

   _____

2. Why is the woman in the poster flexing her muscle?

   _____

   _____

   _____

3. What does the wearing of the bandana and the action of rolling up the sleeve symbolize?

   _____

   _____

   _____

4. On the poster, Rosie the Riveter is dressed in work clothes, has her nails polished, and is wearing cosmetics. What can you infer from her appearance?

   _____

   _____

   _____

Name: _____   Date: _____

Station Four: Making Inferences and Citing Evidence

Directions: Read the excerpts on the "To the Women of Mobile" handout. For each excerpt, make an inference and support it with two pieces of textual evidence.

Excerpt One

Inference:

Evidence:

Evidence:

Excerpt Two

Inference:

Evidence:

Evidence:

Excerpt Three

Inference:

Evidence:

Evidence:

The Nation Mobilizes for War

The day after the attack on Pearl Harbor, long lines gathered in front of recruiting stations, and in Washington, Franklin Delano Roosevelt (FDR) gave an eloquent speech to Congress proclaiming December 7, 1941, a "date which will live in infamy." By a unanimous vote, the Senate voted for war, and only one House member voted against war. The debate over whether the United States should enter the war was over, and very few Americans did not give it full support. As Japanese Admiral Yamamoto had feared when the government decided to attack Pearl Harbor, "We have only awakened a sleeping giant, and his reaction will be terrible."

The United States had begun gearing up for war with the draft (1940) and increased military production (to make the United States what Roosevelt called "the arsenal for democracy"). The president set high, and some said impossible, goals for production, and all of them were exceeded. Factories that had been shut down in 1938 went to eight-hour shifts in 1939, and by 1942, they were turning out products 24 hours a day. In 1938, the United States put out 3,800 aircraft per year; by 1940, that was up to 12,804 aircraft. FDR said that the United States must raise that to 50,000 planes a year. In 1942, 47,000 planes were manufactured, and the next year 85,000 planes came off production lines.

New production techniques were used to build ships. Henry J. Kaiser mass-produced freighters (liberty ships) that could be built by workers in 40 days. By 1945, an aircraft carrier could be built in 16 months, a destroyer in six months.

The War Production Board (WPB) was set up under Donald Nelson to assign where raw materials went, and it coordinated the production of goods needed by the armies and navies, not only of the United States, but of allies as well. Nearly all civilian production stopped so that factories could devote full attention to military needs.

Because scarcity leads to higher prices, the Office of Price Administration (OPA) was created to keep prices in check. Ration books were issued, and when a person bought sugar, gasoline, or any other listed item, they took their billfold and ration book with them. Those with an 'A' sticker on their car were entitled to only four gallons of gasoline a week.

With the 450,000-man military force of 1940 increasing to 9 million in 1943, and with factories rushing to fill orders, the unemployment problem of the late 1930s was reversed. Unemployment running at 19 percent in 1938 dropped to only 1.2 percent in 1944. The labor force included many who had always been excluded before. Women held jobs doing nearly every kind of work men had always done; the symbol of the "new woman" was "Rosie the Riveter," with a bandana around her hair and a riveting machine in her hand.

Elderly people returned to the workforce in record numbers. African-Americans had always found factory jobs closed to them before, but not now; many African-Americans left the south to find work in the north and west.

A sleeping giant had awakened and supplied not only its own troops and sailors but sent thousands of trucks, tanks, and airplanes to other nations. America had indeed become the "arsenal for democracy," and capitalism proved it could produce better than any other system.

(From *U.S. History: People and Events 1865–Present* by George Lee. Used with permission of Mark Twain Media, Inc., Publishers)

We Can Do It! Poster

National Archives
[For a larger or color image go to: <http://media.nara.gov/media/images/20/7/20-0697a.gif>]

To The Women of Mobile

Excerpt One:

"You are needed in the war jobs and in other essential civilian jobs directly aiding the war effort in Mobile NOW. Manpower has been practically exhausted. . . . We must depend upon you—upon womanpower. There are idle machines in war plants which you can operate. There are idle jobs in the shipyards which you can fill. There are jobs in stores, offices, transportation, restaurants, hospitals in which you can render essential war service."

Excerpt Two:

"Women have responded nobly to the call to war service throughout the Nation. Many are employed in the shipyards in Mobile now. Many are at Brookley Field. Still others are in plants which are producing the war supplies essential to victory. Women who have never worked before are employed in stores and other necessary business establishments. Women have proved their efficiency in war work. Throughout our country they are doing work which many believed could be done only by men."

Excerpt Three:

"In the Norfolk navy yards 500 women are employed as mechanics. They operate lathes, serve as drill press operators and shapers, assemble engines, repair radios, generators and electric starters, and are expert welders. The United States Employment Service, after long study, has reported that, 'It can hardly be said that ANY occupation is absolutely unsuitable for the employment of women. Women have shown that they can do or learn to do almost any kind of work.'"

[Excerpts from *War Manpower job flyer promoting women to register for War Jobs., 1942.*; Series: Central Files and Monthly MOPAC Area Reports, compiled 1942–1943; Record Group 211: Records of the War Manpower Commission, 1936–1951; NARA—Southeast Region (Atlanta).]

[For full-text of the document go to: <http://www.archives.gov/southeast/education/resources-by-state/images/wwii-flyer.pdf>]

Teacher Page

Unit: Propaganda Techniques

Goal: Students will be able to identify the most common propaganda and production techniques used in presidential campaign commercials.

Common Core State Standards (CCSS):

6th Grade	7th Grade	8th Grade
RI.6.2. Determine a central idea of a text and how it is conveyed through particular details; provide a summary of the text distinct from personal opinions or judgments.	RI.7.2. Determine two or more central ideas in a text and analyze their development over the course of the text; provide an objective summary of the text.	RI.8.2. Determine a central idea of a text and analyze its development over the course of the text, including its relationship to supporting ideas; provide an objective summary of the text.

© Copyright 2010. National Governors Association Center for Best Practices and Council of Chief State School Officers. All rights reserved.

Materials List/Setup

Station 1*: Presidential Campaign Commercial, 1952 (Activity); Propaganda Techniques (Handout)
Station 2*: Presidential Campaign Commercial, 1960 (Activity); Propaganda Techniques (Handout)
Station 3*: Presidential Campaign Commercial, 1968 (Activity); Propaganda Techniques (Handout)
Station 4*: Presidential Campaign Commercial, 1984 (Activity); Propaganda Techniques (Handout)
Station 5*: Presidential Campaign Commercial, 2004 (Activity); Propaganda Techniques (Handout)

Activity: one copy per student   Handout: one copy per each student in a group

*Integration of Technology Skills and/or Speaking and Listening Standards

Opening Activity and Discussion Questions (Teacher-Directed)

Go online to: <http://www.pbs.org/30secondcandidate/tricks_of_the_trade/>
1. Click on the **ad FOR this candidate** link located at the bottom of the web page and view the different production techniques used with the video.
2. Discussion Question: What production techniques were used to set a positive tone?
3. Click on the **ad AGAINST this candidate** link located at the bottom of the web page.
4. Discussion Question: What production techniques were used to set a negative tone?
5: Discussion Questions: What is propaganda? Why are propaganda techniques used in campaign commercials?

Student Instructions for Learning Stations

At each learning station, you will view a different presidential campaign commercial. On the activity pages, record your observations of the propaganda and production techniques used in the commercials. You may need to view the videos more than one time. Discuss your answers with other team members after completing each activity.

Closure: Reflection

The following questions can be used to stimulate discussion or as a journaling activity.
1. Which campaign commercial did you feel was most effective? Why?
2. Do you think negative campaign commercials should be allowed on television? Explain your answer.

Name: _____ Date: _____

Station One: Presidential Campaign Commercial, 1952

Directions: Go online and watch the campaign video at the web address listed in the graphic organizer. List the propaganda techniques you observe. If you need help, use the Propaganda Techniques handout. Identify the production techniques that were used to set either a positive or negative tone. Cite evidence to support your observations and answers. You may need to view the video more than one time.

Web Address: <http://www.livingroomcandidate.org/commercials/1952/ike-for-president>

Title: "Ike for President"   **Candidate: Dwight D. Eisenhower**   **Year: 1952**

What propaganda technique(s) did you observe?	Cite evidence to support your observations.

Production Techniques	Check if Observed	Did the technique set a positive or negative tone?
Slow motion		
Split screen		
Music		
Voice-over		
Graphics		
Text		
Symbolism		
Sound effects		
Other:		

Name: _____   Date: _____

Station Two: Presidential Campaign Commercial, 1960

Directions: Go online and watch the campaign video at the web address listed in the graphic organizer. List the propaganda techniques you observe. If you need help, use the Propaganda Techniques handout. Identify the production techniques that were used to set either a positive or negative tone. Cite evidence to support your observations and answers. You may need to view the video more than one time.

Web Address: <http://www.livingroomcandidate.org/commercials/1960/jingle>

Title: "Jingle"   **Candidate:** John F. Kennedy   **Year:** 1960

What propaganda technique(s) did you observe?	Cite evidence to support your observations.

Production Techniques	Check if Observed	Did the technique set a positive or negative tone?
Slow motion		
Split screen		
Music		
Voice-over		
Graphics		
Text		
Symbolism		
Sound effects		
Other:		

Name: _____ Date: _____

Station Three: Presidential Campaign Commercial, 1968

Directions: Go online and watch the campaign video at the web address listed in the graphic organizer. List the propaganda techniques you observe. If you need help, use the Propaganda Techniques handout. Identify the production techniques that were used to set either a positive or negative tone. Cite evidence to support your observations and answers. You may need to view the video more than one time.

Web Address: <http://www.livingroomcandidate.org/commercials/1968/bomb-nuclear-treaty>

Title: "Bomb (Nuclear Treaty)"   **Candidate:** Hubert H. Humphrey   **Year:** 1968

What propaganda technique(s) did you observe?	Cite evidence to support your observations.

Production Techniques	Check if Observed	Did the technique set a positive or negative tone?
Slow motion		
Split screen		
Music		
Voice-over		
Graphics		
Text		
Symbolism		
Sound effects		
Other:		

Name: _____ Date: _____

Station Four: Presidential Campaign Commercial, 1984

Directions: Go online and watch the campaign video at the web address listed in the graphic organizer. List the propaganda techniques you observe. If you need help, use the Propaganda Techniques handout. Identify the production techniques that were used to set either a positive or negative tone. Cite evidence to support your observations and answers. You may need to view the video more than one time.

Web Address: <http://www.livingroomcandidate.org/commercials/1984/prouder-stronger-better>

Title: "Prouder, Stronger, Better"   **Candidate: Ronald Reagan**   **Year: 1984**

What propaganda technique(s) did you observe?	Cite evidence to support your observations.

Production Techniques	Check if Observed	Did the technique set a positive or negative tone?
Slow motion		
Split screen		
Music		
Voice-over		
Graphics		
Text		
Symbolism		
Sound effects		
Other:		

Name: _____ Date: _____

Station Five: Presidential Campaign Commercial, 2004

Directions: Go online and watch the campaign video at the web address listed in the graphic organizer. List the propaganda techniques you observe. If you need help, use the Propaganda Techniques handout. Identify the production techniques that were used to set either a positive or negative tone. Cite evidence to support your observations and answers. You may need to view the video more than one time.

Web Address: <http://www.livingroomcandidate.org/commercials/2004/wolves>

Title: "Wolves"   **Candidate:** George W. Bush   **Year:** 2004

What propaganda technique(s) did you observe?	Cite evidence to support your observations.

Production Techniques	Check if Observed	Did the technique set a positive or negative tone?
Slow motion		
Split screen		
Music		
Voice-over		
Graphics		
Text		
Symbolism		
Sound effects		
Other:		

Propaganda Techniques

Propaganda Techniques	What is it? A technique that...	Why is it done? It works because...	Can you give me an example? A political campaign ad...
Bandwagon	tries to persuade other people to "join in" or "do something" because everyone else is.	no one wants to be left out or excluded.	stating "Join with me and other veterans in supporting Candidate A."
Card Stacking	presents the best features or information first and omits the negative.	people tend to think if something sounds logical or feasible it must be true.	stating "As a small business owner, Candidate A has experience creating jobs."
Glittering Generalities	uses positive phrases that appeal to a person's emotions, such as love for country, family, or freedom.	it appeals to our desire for patriotism, basic human goodness, and decency.	describing Candidate A as a family man who supports family values.
Name Calling	connects a negative symbol or label to a person, a group, an idea, or an object.	people form opinions without having all the facts or knowing the accuracy of a claim.	calling Candidate B a wasteful spender in Congress.
Plain Folks	portrays a person as being common, ordinary, or average.	most people can identify with a person who appears to have similar interests and values.	featuring Candidate A doing things like driving a tractor or sitting at a table at a coffee shop.
Repetition	repeats something, such as a message or name, over and over again.	the more times we hear or see something, the easier it is to remember.	featuring a multi-verse campaign song with a chorus.
Testimonial	uses a celebrity or expert to endorse or recommend a person, product, or idea.	we feel we know these people, so they are trustworthy.	featuring a celebrity endorsing Candidate A.
Transfer	takes our feeling for something and transfers it to something else.	we associate positive or negative feelings with people, symbols, or ideas.	displaying an American flag in the background when Candidate A is giving a speech.
Fear	reveals a threat or potential disaster and a choice that would change the outcome.	it invokes feelings of impending doom unless people accept the recommendation.	stating "A vote for Candidate B is a vote to end reliable health care for our children."

Teacher Page

Unit: Organizational Text Structures

Goal: Students will be able to recognize organizational text structures in order to analyze informational text.

Common Core State Standards (CCSS):

6th Grade	7th Grade	8th Grade
RI.6.5. Analyze how a particular sentence, paragraph, chapter, or section fits into the overall structure of a text and contributes to the development of the ideas.	RI.7.5. Analyze the structure an author uses to organize a text, including how the major sections contribute to the whole and to the development of the ideas.	RI.8.5. Analyze in detail the structure of a specific paragraph in a text, including the role of particular sentences in developing and refining a key concept.

© Copyright 2010. National Governors Association Center for Best Practices and Council of Chief State School Officers. All rights reserved.

Materials List/Setup

Station 1: Cause and Effect (Activity); Organizational Text Structures (Handout)
Station 2: Sequential Order (Activity); Organizational Text Structures (Handout)
Station 3: Compare and Contrast (Activity); Organizational Text Structures (Handout)
Station 4: Problem and Solution (Activity); Organizational Text Structures (Handout); editorial sections from newspapers
Station 5: Chronological Order (Activity); Organizational Text Structures (Handout)
Station 6: Description (Activity); Organizational Text Structures (Handout)

Activity: one copy per student
Handout: one copy per each student in a group

Opening Activity and Discussion Questions (Teacher-Directed)

1. What are some examples of text structures used to organize informational text?
2. Why is it important to be able to recognize the text structure used by an author?

Student Instructions for Learning Stations

At the learning stations, you will analyze different types of organizational text structures. Being able to recognize these structures will help you better understand what you read. Discuss your answers with other team members after completing each activity.

Closure: Reflection

The following questions can be used to stimulate discussion or as a journaling activity.
1. Why are text structures used to organize informational text?
2. How does using a graphic organizer help you comprehend the information in a text?

Name: _____ Date: _____

Station One: Cause and Effect

The **cause** is why something happens. The **effect** is the result of what happens.

Directions: Use the information from the passage "A Sleeping Giant Awakes" to complete the graphic organizer.

A Sleeping Giant Awakes

Mount Saint Helens in Washington State, just 50 miles from Portland, Oregon, was a very beautiful mountain. Many felt that the beauty of Mount Saint Helens rivaled that of Mount Fuji in Japan.

Mount Saint Helens had been dormant for 123 years. Then at 8:32 on May 18, 1980, Mount Saint Helens erupted. The explosion blew away about a cubic mile of the mountain and left a huge crater. Sixty people died. High winds spread much of the ash across Washington and Oregon. Hundreds of millions of dollars' worth of land and property were destroyed.

[Adapted from *Disasters* by Don Blattner and Lisa Howerton. Used with permission of Mark Twain Media, Inc., Publishers]

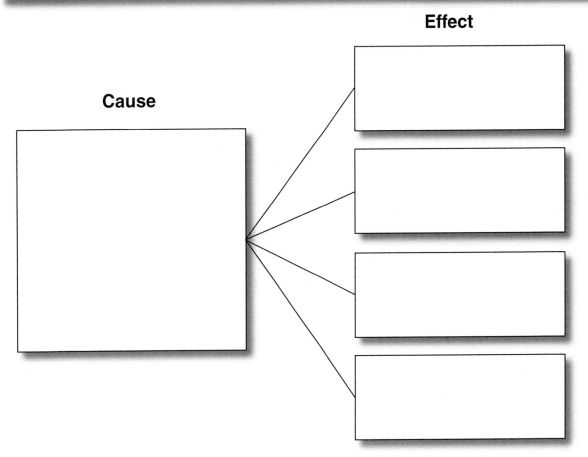

Effect

Cause

Name: _____   Date: _____

Station Two: Sequential Order

Directions: Read the scrambled steps for making a peanut butter and jelly sandwich and brushing your teeth. Number the steps in the correct order.

Steps for Making a Peanut Butter and Jelly Sandwich

Supplies: plastic knife and paper plate
Ingredients: peanut butter, loaf of bread, and jelly

_____ A. Finally, close the sandwich and enjoy!

_____ B. Spread the peanut butter on one slice of bread.

_____ C. Place two slices of bread on the plate.

_____ D. To begin, place the ingredients and supplies needed to make the sandwich on the table in front of you.

_____ E. Then spread the jelly on the other slice of bread.

Steps for Brushing Your Teeth

Supplies: toothbrush, toothpaste, sink, teeth

_____ A. Spit in the sink and rinse your mouth with water.

_____ B. Screw the cap back on the toothpaste tube.

_____ C. Rinse out the sink.

_____ D. Put a pea-sized amount of toothpaste on the toothbrush.

_____ E. Unscrew the lid from the toothpaste tube.

_____ F. Move the toothbrush in an up-and-down motion over your teeth for two minutes.

_____ G. Rinse off the toothbrush.

Name: _____ Date: _____

Station Three: Compare and Contrast

Directions: Read the passage below. Use the information to complete the Venn diagram.

Nonrenewable and Renewable Energy Sources

Every day we use huge amounts of energy to make our lives more comfortable and to operate machines. The energy we use comes from natural resources (resources supplied by nature).

Most of the world's energy comes from nonrenewable energy sources. These sources are limited and cannot be replaced in a timely manner by natural processes. Most nonrenewable energy is used to make electricity and liquid fuels, like gasoline. Coal, petroleum, natural gas, propane, and uranium are nonrenewable energy sources. These resources come from the ground.

Renewable energy sources are not limited and can be replaced by natural processes. We use renewable energy sources mainly to make electricity. Renewable energy sources include biomass, geothermal, hydropower, solar, ocean, and wind.

[Adapted from *Alternative Energy Experiments* by Schyrlet Cameron and Carolyn Craig. Used with permission of Mark Twain Media, Inc., Publishers]

Comparison of Renewable and Nonrenewable Energy Sources

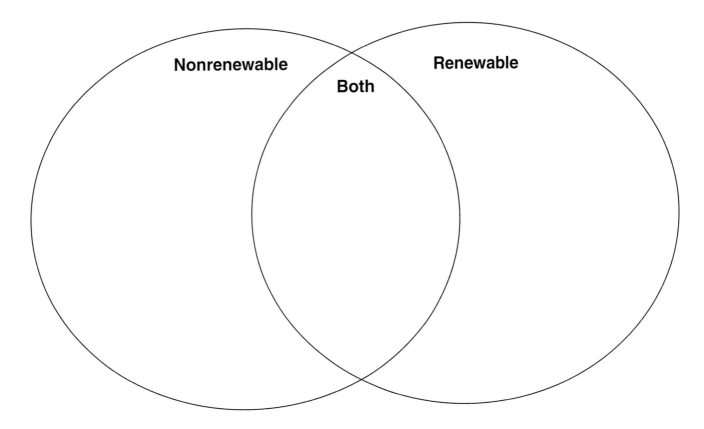

Name: _____ Date: _____

Station Four: Problem and Solution

An **editorial** is an opinion piece written by the senior editorial staff or publisher of a newspaper.

Directions: Find a newspaper editorial where the author has used the problem/solution structure. Complete the graphic organizer for the editorial.

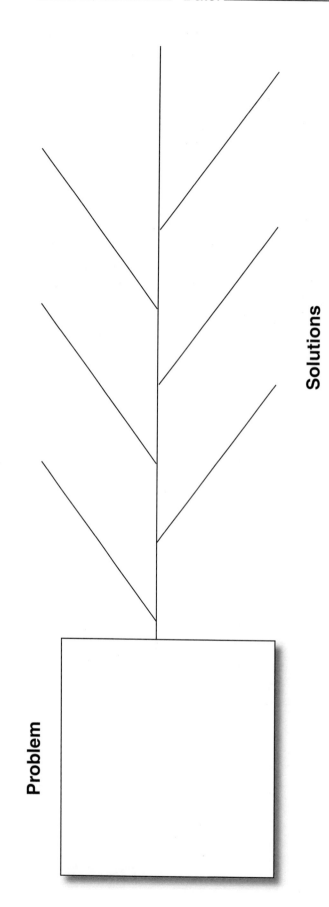

Problem

Solutions

Name: _____ Date: _____

Station Four: Chronological Order

A **time line** is a graphic organizer used to present events in chronological order.

Directions: Fill in the time line with seven important events in your life. Start the time line with your birth.

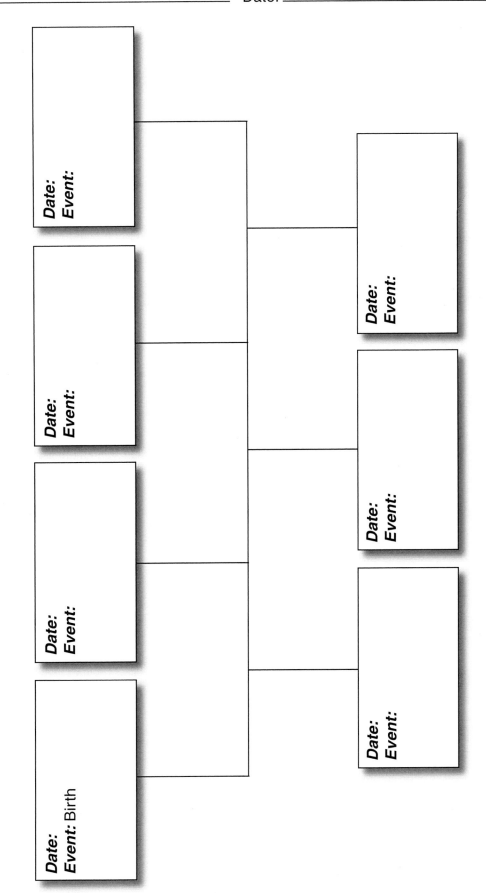

Date:
Event:

Date:
Event:

Date:
Event:

Date:
Event: Birth

Date:
Event:

Date:
Event:

Date:
Event:

Name: _____ Date: _____

Station Six: Description

Directions: Read the passage below. Use the information to complete the graphic organizer.

Eight

~~Nine~~ Planets

The sun, planets, asteroid belt, comets, and meteoroids make up our solar system. Scientists once believed there were nine planets in our solar system, and Pluto was the farthest planet from the Sun. Pluto is a cold, dense celestial body over 3.5 billion miles from the Sun. It was considered the smallest of the nine planets. Pluto has a diameter of 1,484 miles and is smaller than Earth's moon. Pluto is so far away from Earth that little is known about it. Even the Hubble Space Telescope can make out only the largest features on its surface. In 2006, because of its small size and eccentric orbit, the International Astronomical Union (IAU) formally reclassified Pluto as a dwarf planet.

[Adapted from *Astronomy: Our Solar System and Beyond* by Don Powers and John B. Beaver. Used with permission of Mark Twain Media, Inc., Publishers]

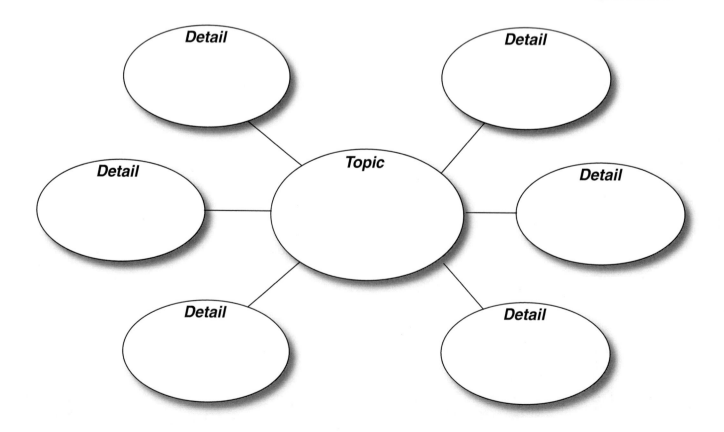

Common Organizational Text Structures

Text structures are organizational patterns used to break information down into parts that can be easily understood by the reader. Knowing the key words and phrases used to signal the use of a particular organizational text structure can help you focus your attention on key concepts and better understand what you are reading.

Comparison/Contrast examines how concepts and events are alike and different. **Signal Words:** alike, different, same, similar, both, compare to	**Classification** divides topics into related categories or groups. **Signal Words:** group, divide, sort, classify, type
Definition introduces and explains a word or concept. **Signal Words:** is, for example, also, can be, defined, in fact	**Cause/Effect** presents a major idea or event and resulting effects. **Signal words:** because of, as a result of, may be due to, causing, therefore
Description describes something using details and/or examples. **Signal Words:** appears to be, for instance, for example, such as, looks like	**Argument/Support** states a point of view and supports it with details or evidence. **Signal Words:** I believe, in my opinion, I think
Chronological/Sequential arranges information into chronological order or is a list of steps in a process. **Signal Words:** first, next, then, now, before, after, last, finally	**Problem/Solution** states a problem and gives possible solutions. **Signal Words:** question is, answer is, the problem is, to solve this, one idea is

Teacher Page

Unit: Text Features

Goal: Students will be able to identify the different types of text features.

Common Core State Standards (CCSS):

6th Grade	7th Grade	8th Grade
RI.6.5. Analyze how a particular sentence, paragraph, chapter, or section fits into the overall structure of a text and contributes to the development of the ideas.	RI.7.5. Analyze the structure an author uses to organize a text, including how the major sections contribute to the whole and to the development of the ideas.	RI.8.5. Analyze in detail the structure of a specific paragraph in a text, including the role of particular sentences in developing and refining a key concept.

© Copyright 2010. National Governors Association Center for Best Practices and Council of Chief State School Officers. All rights reserved.

Materials List/Setup

Station 1: Organizational Text Features (Activity); textbooks

Station 2: Print Features (Activity); magazines, markers, scissors, and glue

Teacher Directions: Cover a large area of the wall with roll paper. Using a marker, divide the paper into box-like sections. Label each box with the name of a text feature.

Station 3: Text Mapping (Activity); text-mapping scroll for each team; different colored markers

Teacher Directions: How to Make a Text-Mapping Scroll—Take apart an old social studies or science textbook. Divide the pages into equal sections for each team. Tape or glue the pages of each section together to make a horizontal scroll.

Station 4: Graphic Text Features (Activity); variety of nonfiction and reference books, magazines, and newspapers

Activity: one copy per student

Opening Activity and Discussion Questions (Teacher-Directed)

1. What are text features?
2. What do text features tell you about the type of text you are reading?

Student Instructions for Learning Stations

At the learning stations, you will examine informational text for the usage of text features. Discuss your answers with other team members after completing each activity.

Closure: Reflection

The following questions can be used to stimulate discussion or as a journaling activity.
1. Which informational text features do you see used most often in your textbooks?
2. Which print feature do you find most helpful?

Name: _____ Date: _____

Station One: Organizational Text Features

Organizational text features are designed to help you locate information in a book. Most textbooks have three basic organizational features: table of contents, index, and glossary.

Table of Contents	Index	Glossary
The **table of contents** is a list of the major parts of a book and the starting page numbers.	The **index** is an alphabetical list of topics and the page numbers where the information can be found.	A **glossary** is an alphabetical list of important words with definitions and pronunciations.

Directions: Use a textbook to answer the questions below.

Title: _____

Index

1. Beginning page number _____ Ending page number _____

2. What is the name of a subject that has several pages of information listed? _____

   _____

3. What is the name of a subject that has only a single page listed? _____

   _____

Table of Contents

4. Where is the table of contents located (front, middle, back)? _____

5. How many chapters are listed? _____

6. What is the title of the first chapter? _____

Glossary

7. What type of information can be found for each word entry? _____

   _____

8. In the chart below, list two words from the glossary that are familiar, two words that are unfamiliar, and the page number where each word is used first.

Familiar Word	Page Number	Unfamiliar Word	Page Number

Name: _____ Date: _____

Station Two: Print Features

An author uses **print features** to signal when a word, phrase, or idea is important. Print features are intended to focus your attention on the text and help you determine the importance of the information.

Directions: Cut examples of print features from a magazine. Glue the items inside the correct box on the wall chart located at your station.

Print Features

Features	Definitions	Purpose
Heading	the title of the text	helps the reader find main ideas and topics
Subheading	a heading given to a section of text	helps the reader navigate the text
Bold/Color	text printed darker or in color	signals the word is important or found in the glossary
Italic	a style of printing where letters slant to the right	distinguishes words from other words in the text
Font	the type and size of the text	helps with readability and creates a mood
Bullet	a symbol such as a dot	emphasizes a list of items
Asterisk	a small star-like symbol	indicates an omission or reference to a footnote
Caption	phrase or sentence(s) usually found under or near an illustration	explains what is shown in an illustration

Name: _____ Date: _____

Station Three: Text Mapping

Text mapping is a graphic organizer technique. It can be used to help with reading comprehension and writing skills. A scroll of pages is created from an old textbook. Then the different text features are marked or highlighted on the scroll. Labels and notes about the text features can also be added. This helps highlight the important features in the text.

Directions: Work as a team to complete the station activity. Unroll one of the text-mapping scrolls on a flat surface. Use different colored markers to highlight, circle, draw a box around, or othewise mark the different text features located on the scroll. If you need help, use the chart below.

For example, use one color for headings and a different color for subheadings. Then, draw a box around all the text that goes with each heading or subheading. This helps you visualize the text as different chunks of information about each topic. Write labels on the scroll identifying each type of text feature, such as maps, sidebars, table of contents, bold print, or bullet points.

Purpose of Text Features		
Organizes Information	**Signals Important Information**	**Expands Meaning of Text**
• table of contents • index • glossary • appendix	• titles • headings • subheadings • bold or highlighted print • italics • underlining • font • bullet	• illustrations • sidebar • maps • chart/tables • time line

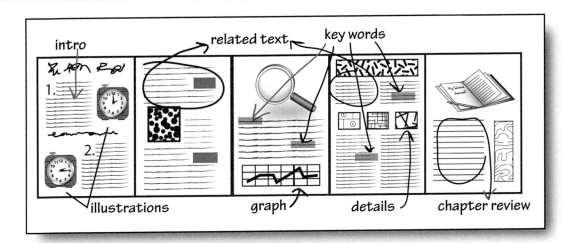

Name: _____   Date: _____

Station Four: Graphic Text Features

Directions: Look through books, magazines, and newspapers to find an example for each graphic text feature listed below. Complete the graphic organizer by writing the title of the resource and page number where the text feature was found.

Illustration	Chart/Table	Map	Sidebar	Diagram	Time Line	Graph
An illustration is a visual way to give information. Photographs, drawings, and sketches are examples of illustrations.	Charts and tables are graphic organizers used to summarize or compare information.	A map is a representation of the earth's surface.	A sidebar is a boxed section off to the side of the main text; contains related information.	A diagram is a labeled drawing that shows or explains something.	A time line is a graphic organizer used to show important events in chronological order.	A graph is a diagram displaying numerical information.

	Illustration	Chart/Table	Map	Sidebar	Diagram	Time Line	Graph
Title of Resource							
Page Number							

Teacher Page

Unit: Bias and Point of View

Goal: Students will be able to identify bias and point of view in informational texts.

Common Core State Standards (CCSS):

6th Grade	7th Grade	8th Grade
RI.6.6. Determine an author's point of view or purpose in a text and explain how it is conveyed in the text.	RI.7.6. Determine an author's point of view or purpose in a text and analyze how the author distinguishes his or her position from that of others.	RI.8.6. Determine an author's point of view or purpose in a text and analyze how the author acknowledges and responds to conflicting evidence or viewpoints.

© Copyright 2010. National Governors Association Center for Best Practices and Council of Chief State School Officers. All rights reserved.

Materials List/Setup

Station 1: Bias (Activity); newspapers
Station 2: Loaded Words (Activity); magazines
Station 3: Point of View (Activity); letters to the editor from newspapers and magazines
Station 4: Bias and Point of View (Activity); Letter to John D. Johnston. Shelbyville. November 4, 1851 (Handout)

Activity: one copy per student
Handout: one copy per each student in a group

Opening Activity and Discussion Questions (Teacher-Directed)

1. Why do some people believe everything they hear or read?
2. Have you ever heard the terms "slanted" or "biased"? What do they mean?

Student Instructions for Learning Stations

At the learning stations, you will analyze a text to determine the author's point of view and bias. Discuss your answers with other team members after completing each activity.

Closure: Reflection

The following questions can be used to stimulate discussion or as a journaling activity.
1. When reading informational text, why is it important to know an author's background or qualifications?
2. What are some indicators of bias?
   [Possible answers: A writer will use all positive or all negative words. The argument appeals more to the emotions than to logic.]

Name: _____ Date: _____

Station One: Bias

Bias is to favor one point of view over another. Many times authors show their bias through word choice. To evaluate what you are reading, you need to be able to recognize bias.

Part A

Directions: Look for bias in the headlines below.

1. Which headline (A or B) shows bias for the Cardinals? _____

   How do you know? _____

   _____

A.

B.

Part B

Directions: Cut out a headline from a newspaper article. Use the headline to answer the questions below. Attach the headline to this paper.

1. Read the headline. What do you predict the article is about? _____

   _____

2. What words in the headline helped you with your prediction? _____

   _____

3. Does the headline contain bias? Cite details from the headline to support your answer.

   _____

   _____

Name: _____   Date: _____

Station Two: Loaded Words

Businesses use bias, or personal opinions and attitudes, to try and sell their products or services. In their advertisements, they use **loaded words** with positive connotations in order to influence consumers.

Directions: Look through magazines to find five advertisements. Complete the chart for each advertisement. An example has been provided.

Product Name	Loaded Words	The loaded words cause the consumer to believe ...
Orion Luxury Sedan	Luxurious, fully loaded, plush	owning this car means that you are wealthier than your neighbors

Name: _____ Date: _____

Station Three: Point of View

Readers of magazines and newspapers sometimes send letters to the editor in order to share their opinion on an issue. The author of the letter presents an argument to support his or her **point of view**.

Directions: Select a letter to the editor from a magazine or newspaper. After reading the letter, complete the graphic organizer.

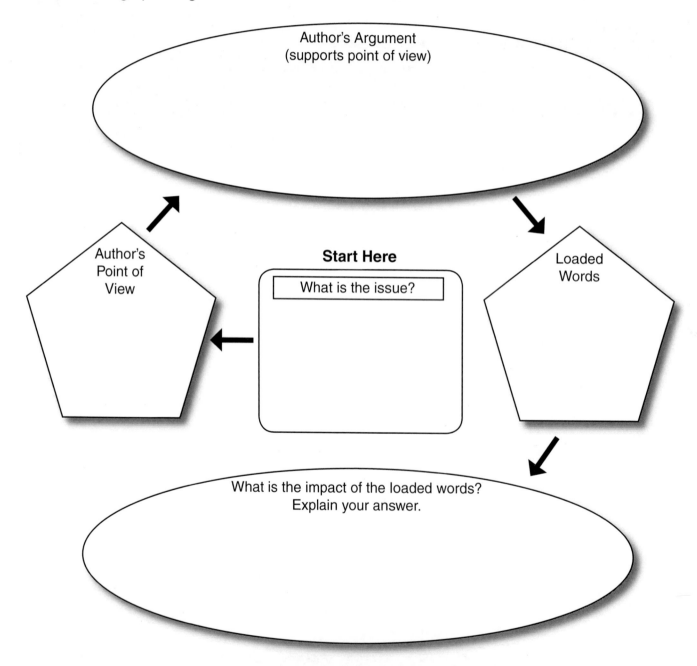

Teacher Page

Unit: Comparing Text and Media

Goal: Students will be able to compare and contrast the different formats used to present information.

Common Core State Standards (CCSS):

6th Grade	7th Grade	8th Grade
RI.6.7. Integrate information presented in different media or formats (e.g., visually, quantitatively) as well as in words to develop a coherent understanding of a topic or issue.	RI.7.7. Compare and contrast a text to an audio, video, or multimedia version of the text, analyzing each medium's portrayal of the subject (e.g., how the delivery of a speech affects the impact of the words).	RI.8.7. Evaluate the advantages and disadvantages of using different mediums (e.g., print or digital text, video, multimedia) to present a particular topic or idea.

© Copyright 2010. National Governors Association Center for Best Practices and Council of Chief State School Officers. All rights reserved.

Materials List/Setup

Station 1*: Public Speaking: Tone (Activity)
Station 2*: Public Speaking: Mood (Activity)
Station 3*: Evaluation of Media Types (Activity); Transcript of John F. Kennedy Inaugural Address, January 20, 1961 (Handout)
Station 4*: Nonverbal Communication

Activity: one copy per student
Handout: one copy per each student in a group

*Integration of Technology Skills and/or Speaking and Listening Standards

Opening Activity and Discussion Questions (Teacher-Directed)

1. Have you ever watched a president give an inaugural address?
2. What is the purpose of the speech?

Student Instructions for Learning Stations

At the learning stations, you will use the inaugural speeches of Abraham Lincoln and John F. Kennedy to evaluate how text is presented in different formats and its impact on the audience. Discuss your answers with other team members after completing each activity.

Closure: Reflection

The following questions can be used to stimulate discussion or as a journaling activity.
1. What are the advantages of using video to present information?
2. Does the delivery of a speech influence how you feel about the speaker or topic?

Letter to John D Johnston. Shelbyville. November 4, 1851

Dear Brother, When I came into Charleston day before yesterday, I learned that you are anxious to sell the land where you live and move to Missouri. I have been thinking of this ever since, and cannot but think such a notion is utterly foolish. What can you do in Missouri better than here? Is the land any richer? Can you there, any more than here, raise corn and wheat and oats without work? Will anybody there, any more than here, do your work for you? If you intend to go to work, there is no better place than right where you are; if you do not intend to go to work, you cannot get along anywhere. Squirming and crawling about from place to place can do no good. You have raised no crop this year; and what you really want is to sell the land, get the money, and spend it. Part with the land you have, and, my life upon it, you will never after own a spot big enough to bury you in. Half you will get for the land you will spend in moving to Missouri, and the other half you will eat, drink, and wear out, and no foot of land will be bought. Now, I feel it my duty to have no hand in such a piece of foolery. I feel that it is so even on your own account, and particularly on mother's account. The eastern forty acres I intend to keep for mother while she lives; if you will not cultivate it, it will rent for enough to support her—at least, it will rent for something. Her dower in the other two forties she can let you have, and no thanks to me. Now, do not misunderstand this letter; I do not write it in any unkindness. I write it in order, if possible, to get you to face the truth, which truth is, you are destitute because you have idled away all your time. Your thousand pretences for not getting along better are all nonsense; they deceive nobody but yourself. Go to work is the only cure for your case.

A word to mother. Chapman tells me he wants you to go and live with him. If I were you I would try it awhile. If you get tired of it (as I think you will not), you can return to your own home. Chapman feels very kindly to you, and I have no doubt he will make your situation very pleasant.

[Excerpt from *Speeches & Letters of Abraham Lincoln, 1832–1865*, edited by Merwin Roe. 1912.]

Teacher Page

Unit: Comparing Text and Media

Goal: Students will be able to identify bias and point of view in informational texts.

Common Core State Standards (CCSS):

6th Grade	7th Grade	8th Grade
RI.6.7. Integrate information presented in different media or formats (e.g., visually, quantitatively) as well as in words to develop a coherent understanding of a topic or issue.	RI.7.7. Compare and contrast a text to an audio, video, or multimedia version of the text, analyzing each medium's portrayal of the subject (e.g., how the delivery of a speech affects the impact of the words).	RI.8.7. Evaluate the advantages and disadvantages of using different mediums (e.g., print or digital text, video, multimedia) to present a particular topic or idea.

© Copyright 2010. National Governors Association Center for Best Practices and Council of Chief State School Officers. All rights reserved.

Materials List/Setup

Station 1*: Public Speaking: Tone (Activity)
Station 2*: Public Speaking: Mood (Activity)
Station 3*: Evaluation of Media Types (Activity); Transcript of John F. Kennedy Inaugural Address, January 20, 1961 (Handout)
Station 4*: Nonverbal Communication

Activity: one copy per student
Handout: one copy per each student in a group

*Integration of Technology Skills and/or Speaking and Listening Standards

Opening Activity and Discussion Questions (Teacher-Directed)

1. Have you ever watched a president give an inaugural address?
2. What is the purpose of the speech?

Student Instructions for Learning Stations

At the learning stations, you will use the inaugural speeches of Abraham Lincoln and John F. Kennedy to evaluate how text is presented in different formats and its impact on the audience. Discuss your answers with other team members after completing each activity.

Closure: Reflection

The following questions can be used to stimulate discussion or as a journaling activity.
1. What are the advantages of using video to present information?
2. Does the delivery of a speech influence how you feel about the speaker or topic?

Name: _____ Date: _____

Station One: Public Speaking: Tone

In the midst of the Civil War, Abraham Lincoln delivered his second inaugural address in Washington, D.C. on March 4, 1865.

Directions: On the text of the speech below, highlight any words you think Abraham Lincoln would have emphasized to the audience. Pair up with another student on your team. Take turns presenting your own dramatic interpretations of the inaugural address. Demonstrate public-speaking skills (e.g., voice level, tone, gestures, and dramatic pause) necessary to communicate effectively with an audience.

Abraham Lincoln's Second Inaugural Address

On the occasion corresponding to this four years ago, all thoughts were anxiously directed to an impending civil war. All dreaded it,—all sought to avert it. While the inaugural address was being delivered from this place, devoted altogether to saving the Union without war, insurgent agents were in the city seeking to destroy it without war,—seeking to dissolve the Union, and divide effects, by negotiation. Both parties deprecated war; but one of them would make war rather than let the nation survive, and the other would accept war rather than let it perish. And the war came.

One-eighth of the whole population were coloured slaves, not distributed generally over the Union, but localized in the southern part of it. These slaves constituted a peculiar and powerful interest. All knew that this interest was, somehow, the cause of the war. To strengthen, perpetuate, and extend this interest was the object for which the insurgents would rend the Union, even by war; while the government claimed no right to do more than to restrict the territorial enlargement of it . . . .

With malice toward none; with charity for all; with firmness in the right, as God gives us to see the right,—let us strive on to finish the work we are in: to bind up the nation's wounds; to care for him who shall have borne the battle, and for his widow and his orphan; to do all which may achieve and cherish a just and lasting peace among ourselves, and with all nations.

[Excerpt from *Speeches & Letters of Abraham Lincoln, 1832–1865.* edited by Merwin Roe. 1912.]

How did your delivery of the speech differ from your partner's delivery of the speech?

_____

_____

_____

_____

Name: _____ Date: _____

Station Two: Public Speaking: Mood

Directions: Go online to: <http://memory.loc.gov/service/pnp/ppmsc/02900/02928v.jpg>. The primary source is a photograph of Abraham Lincoln delivering his second inaugural address on March 4, 1865. Examine the photograph closely. Look at the picture as a whole, then focus on the individual details. Record your observations in the graphic organizer below. Then use your observations to answer the question.

Detail (What I Observe)	This leads me to question...	Inference (My Best Guess)

What do you think the audience's reaction was to Lincoln's speech? Use your observations to support your answer. _____

_____

_____

_____

Name: _____   Date: _____

Station Three: Evaluation of Media Types

Web Address: <http://www.jfklibrary.org/Asset-Viewer/Archives/USG-17.aspx>
Title: Inaugural Address, 20 January 1961
Source: John F. Kennedy Presidential Library and Museum

Directions: Follow the steps below.

Step 1: (Text): Read the handout "John F. Kennedy Inaugural Address, January 20, 1961," located on page 42. Then list the advantages and disadvantages of reading the text format of the speech.

Step 2: (Audio): Go online to the above web address. After pressing play, cover up your screen and listen to President Kennedy deliver his inaugural address. Then list the advantages and disadvantages of listening to the audio presentation.

Step 3: (Video): At the same web address is the video of President John F. Kennedy delivering his inaugural address. View the video presentation of the speech. Then list the advantages and disadvantages of watching the video presentation.

Format Type	Advantages	Disadvantages
Text		
Audio		
Video		

Name: _____ Date: _____

Station Four: Nonverbal Communication

Web Address: <http://www.jfklibrary.org/Asset-Viewer/Archives/USG-17.aspx>
Title: Inaugural Address, 20 January 1961
Source: John F. Kennedy Presidential Library and Museum

Directions: View the online video of President John F. Kennedy delivering his inaugural address. In the graphic organizer, record your observations of his nonverbal communication during the beginning, middle, and end of the speech.

Items to Observe	Observations of Nonverbal Communication		
	Beginning of Speech	**Middle of Speech**	**End of Speech**
Gestures (e.g. hand, arm, head)			
Facial Expressions			
Eye Contact			
Posture			

1. Did President Kennedy's nonverbal communication change during the speech? Use your observations to support your answer. _____

_____

_____

_____

2. Did the use of nonverbal communication have an impact on the audience? Explain your answer. _____

_____

_____

_____

John F. Kennedy Inaugural Address, January 20, 1961
(Transcript)

Web Address: <http://www.jfklibrary.org/Asset-Viewer/Archives/JFKPOF-034-002.aspx>
Title: Inaugural Address, 20 January 1961
Source: John F. Kennedy Presidential Library and Museum

(01:11) 1 *Vice President Johnson, Mr. Speaker, Mr. Chief Justice, President Eisenhower, Vice President Nixon, President Truman, Reverend Clergy, fellow citizens:*

(01:30) 2 We observe today not a victory of party but a celebration of freedom—symbolizing an end as well as a beginning—signifying renewal as well as change. For I have sworn before you and Almighty God the same solemn oath our forbears prescribed nearly a century and three-quarters ago.

(02:02) 3 The world is very different now. For man holds in his mortal hands the power to abolish all forms of human poverty and all forms of human life. And yet the same revolutionary beliefs for which our forebears fought are still at issue around the globe—the belief that the rights of man come not from the generosity of the state but from the hand of God.

(02:39) 4 We dare not forget today that we are the heirs of that first revolution. Let the word go forth from this time and place, to friend and foe alike, that the torch has been passed to a new generation of Americans—born in this century, tempered by war, disciplined by a hard and bitter peace, proud of our ancient heritage—and unwilling to witness or permit the slow undoing of those human rights to which this nation has always been committed, and to which we are committed today at home and around the world.

(03:39) 5 Let every nation know, whether it wishes us well or ill, that we shall pay any price, bear any burden, meet any hardship, support any friend, oppose any foe to assure the survival and the success of liberty.

(04:10) 6 This much we pledge—and more.

(04:13) 7 To those old allies whose cultural and spiritual origins we share, we pledge the loyalty of faithful friends. United there is little we cannot do in a host of cooperative ventures. Divided there is little we can do—for we dare not meet a powerful challenge at odds and split asunder.

(04:42) 8 To those new states whom we welcome to the ranks of the free, we pledge our word that one form of colonial control shall not have passed away merely to be replaced by a far more iron tyranny. We shall not always expect to find them supporting our view. But we shall always hope to find them strongly supporting their own freedom—and to remember that, in the past, those who foolishly sought power by riding the back of the tiger ended up inside.

John F. Kennedy Inaugural Address (cont.)

(05:31) 9 To those people in the huts and villages of half the globe struggling to break the bonds of mass misery, we pledge our best efforts to help them help themselves, for whatever period is required—not because the communists may be doing it, not because we seek their votes, but because it is right. If a free society cannot help the many who are poor, it cannot save the few who are rich.

(06:13) 10 To our sister republics south of our border, we offer a special pledge—to convert our good words into good deeds—in a new alliance for progress—to assist free men and free governments in casting off the chains of poverty. But this peaceful revolution of hope cannot become the prey of hostile powers. Let all our neighbors know that we shall join with them to oppose aggression or subversion anywhere in the Americas. And let every other power know that this Hemisphere intends to remain the master of its own house.

(07:11) 11 To that world assembly of sovereign states, the United Nations, our last best hope in an age where the instruments of war have far outpaced the instruments of peace, we renew our pledge of support—to prevent it from becoming merely a forum for invective—to strengthen its shield of the new and the weak—and to enlarge the area in which its writ may run.

(07:44) 12 Finally, to those nations who would make themselves our adversary, we offer not a pledge but a request: that both sides begin anew the quest for peace, before the dark powers of destruction unleashed by science engulf all humanity in planned or accidental self-destruction.

(08:15) 13 We dare not tempt them with weakness. For only when our arms are sufficient beyond doubt can we be certain beyond doubt that they will never be employed.

(08:29) 14 But neither can two great and powerful groups of nations take comfort from our present course—both sides overburdened by the cost of modern weapons, both rightly alarmed by the steady spread of the deadly atom, yet both racing to alter that uncertain balance of terror that stays the hand of mankind's final war.

(09:00) 15 So let us begin anew—remembering on both sides that civility is not a sign of weakness, and sincerity is always subject to proof. Let us never negotiate out of fear. But let us never fear to negotiate.

(09:26) 16 Let both sides explore what problems unite us instead of belaboring those problems which divide us.

(09:35) 17 Let both sides, for the first time, formulate serious and precise proposals for the inspection and control of arms—and bring the absolute power to destroy other nations under the absolute control of all nations.

(09:59) 18 Let both sides seek to invoke the wonders of science instead of its terrors. Together let us explore the stars, conquer the deserts, eradicate disease, tap the ocean depths and encourage the arts and commerce.

John F. Kennedy Inaugural Address (cont.)

(10:20) 19 Let both sides unite to heed in all corners of the earth the command of Isaiah—to "undo the heavy burdens . . . (and) let the oppressed go free."

(10:35) 20 And if a beachhead of cooperation may push back the jungle of suspicion, let both sides join in creating a new endeavor, not a new balance of power, but a new world of law, where the strong are just and the weak secure and the peace preserved.

(11:00) 21 All this will not be finished in the first one hundred days. Nor will it be finished in the first one thousand days, nor in the life of this Administration, nor even perhaps in our lifetime on this planet. But let us begin.

(11:28) 22 In your hands, my fellow citizens, more than mine, will rest the final success or failure of our course. Since this country was founded, each generation of Americans has been summoned to give testimony to its national loyalty. The graves of young Americans who answered the call to service surround the globe.

(11:59) 23 Now the trumpet summons us again—not as a call to bear arms, though arms we need— not as a call to battle, though embattled we are—but a call to bear the burden of a long twilight struggle, year in and year out, "rejoicing in hope, patient in tribulation"—a struggle against the common enemies of man: tyranny, poverty, disease and war itself.

(12:38) 24 Can we forge against these enemies a grand and global alliance, North and South, East and West, that can assure a more fruitful life for all mankind? Will you join in that historic effort?

(13:05) 25 In the long history of the world, only a few generations have been granted the role of defending freedom in its hour of maximum danger. I do not shrink from this responsibility—I welcome it. I do not believe that any of us would exchange places with any other people or any other generation. The energy, the faith, the devotion which we bring to this endeavor will light our country and all who serve it—and the glow from that fire can truly light the world.

(13:54) 26 And so, my fellow Americans: ask not what your country can do for you—ask what you can do for your country.

(14:12) 27 My fellow citizens of the world: ask not what America will do for you, but what together we can do for the freedom of man.

(14:29) 28 Finally, whether you are citizens of America or citizens of the world, ask of us here the same high standards of strength and sacrifice which we ask of you. With a good conscience our only sure reward, with history the final judge of our deeds, let us go forth to lead the land we love, asking His blessing and His help, but knowing that here on earth God's work must truly be our own.

Answer Keys

*If applicable, answers are provided.

Unit: Inferences and Evidence
Citing Textual Evidence (p. 4)
Answers will vary.
Question A: factories that had been shut down in 1938 went to eight-hour shifts in 1939; by 1942 they were turning out products 24 hours a day; new production techniques were used to build ships; War Production Board was set up to assign where raw materials went
Question B: women held jobs doing most every kind of work men had always done; elderly people returned to the workforce; African-Americans had always found factory jobs closed to them before, but not now

Evaluating Textual Evidence (p. 5)
Question #1: A, C, D, E, I
Question #2: D, F, G, J
Not: B, H

Making Inferences: Poster (p. 6)
Answers will vary.
1. Women were capable of doing the jobs that men had once held.
2. This type of pose is usually done to show strength. It conveys that women have the strength to go to work outside the home.
3. Women were ready to work.
4. Women can do the work of men and still retain their femininity.

Unit: Propaganda Techniques (p. 12–16)
Answers will vary. Teacher check.

Unit: Organizational Text Structures
Cause and Effect (p. 19)
Cause: eruption of Mount Saint Helens
Effects: left a huge crater; sixty people died; ash spread across Washington and Oregon; land and property destroyed

Sequential Order (p. 20)
Peanut Butter and Jelly Sandwich: A. 5
B. 3   C. 2   D. 1   E. 4
Brushing Your Teeth: A. 5   B. 3
C. 7   D. 2   E. 1   F. 4   G. 6

Compare and Contrast (p. 21)
Nonrenewable: limited; can't be replaced in a timely manner; used to make liquid fuels; comes from the ground; coal, petroleum, natural gas, propane, uranium
Both: energy sources; used to generate electricity; makes our lives more comfortable; used to operate machines
Renewable: not limited; can be replaced in a timely manner; biomass, geothermal, hydropower, solar, ocean, wind

Description (p. 24)
Answers will vary.
Topic: Pluto
Details: cold; dense; celestial body; over 3.5 billion miles away from the sun; 1,484 miles in diameter; smaller than Earth's moon; has an eccentric orbit; now reclassified as a dwarf planet

Unit: Text Features (p. 27–30)
Answers will vary. Teacher check.

Unit: Bias and Point of View
Bias (p. 32)
Part A
1. Headline A; It uses a more forceful verb (crush) and an exclamation point.
Part B
Answers will vary.

Bias and Point of View (p. 35)

1. He thought his brother was foolish for trying to sell the land and move. Evidence: I have been thinking of this ever since, and cannot but think such a notion is utterly foolish.

2. Answers may vary. His brother will spend his money from the sale of the land and will never own land again. Evidence: Part with the land you have, and, my life upon it, you will never after own a spot big enough to bury you in. Half you will get for the land you will spend in moving to Missouri, and the other half you will eat, drink, and wear out, and no foot of land will be bought.

3. Answers may include: anxious; foolish; it is my duty; foolery; idled; pretences; nonsense; deceive

4. Answers will vary.

Unit: Comparing Text and Media (p. 38–41)
Answers will vary. Teacher check.